Narcissist

A Complete Guide to Dealing with a Range of Narcissistic Personalities

By Victor Murphy

Legal Disclaimer

The information contained in this book and its contents is not designed to replace any form of medical or professional advice; and is not meant to replace the need for independent medical, financial, legal, or other professional advice or services that may be required. The content and information in this book have been provided for educational and entertainment purposes only.

The content and information contained in this book have been compiled from sources deemed reliable, and they are accurate to the best of the Author's knowledge, information, and belief. However, the Author cannot guarantee its accuracy and validity and therefore cannot be held liable for any errors and/or omissions. Further, changes are periodically made to this book as needed. Where appropriate and/or necessary, you must consult a professional (including but not limited to your doctor, attorney, financial advisor, or other such professional) before using any of the suggested remedies, techniques, and/or information in this book.

Upon using this book's contents and information, you agree to hold harmless the Author from any damages, costs, and expenses, including any legal fees, potentially resulting from the application of any of the information in this book. This disclaimer applies to any loss, damages, or injury caused by the use and application of this book's contents, whether directly or indirectly, whether for breach of contract, tort, negligence, personal injury, criminal intent, or under any other circumstance.

You agree to accept all risks of using the information presented in this book.

You agree that by continuing to read this book, where appropriate and/or necessary, you shall consult a professional (including but not limited to your doctor, attorney, financial advisor, or other such professional) before using any of the suggested remedies, techniques, or information in this book.

Table of Contents

Introduction

We hear so many buzz words, seemingly on a daily basis, and one you will no doubt have heard thrown around quite commonly is 'narcissist', or 'narcissism'. These are of course one and the same thing.

This book is going to talk about this very subject and highlight the fact that whilst you might feel like you meet narcissists every single day of your life, a genuine narcissist is actually quite rare. What you're probably encountering is a person who has a generally inflated sense of self-importance, but one trait alone doesn't diagnose someone with a narcissistic tendency!

The thing is, most people have a slight narcissist tendency at some point in their lives. Sometimes we can be over-confident, sometimes we can put others down needlessly, and sometimes we can seek out validation for no reason. None of this means that we are a narcissist, unless there are several traits together, and it happens on a very regular basis.

You see, a true narcissist is actually a person who needs help, but the problem is that most of them will never admit they need it, and so therefore never really receive it. It's a sad fact, but one which is all too common. Narcissists, real ones, are actually rare, with the Diagnostic and Statistical Manual of Mental Disorders stating that between 0.5% - 1% of the US population has true narcissism, e.g. they have been diagnosed with Narcissistic Personality Disorder (more on that shortly). Within that, between half to three quarters are men. Of course, women can be equally as narcissistic, but it seems that more men display these traits on a regular basis.

Dealing with a narcissist, especially if you find yourself growing close to one, can be a very difficult situation to be in. You probably won't realize that they are actually narcissistic until you do grow close, because these types of people are masters of disguise. They will appear charming, aloof, and extremely attentive until they have you hooked. From then on, the traits appear, and emotional manipulation takes hold.

No, a narcissist isn't an evil person. A narcissist is someone who suffers from a genuine personality disorder. Despite that, it doesn't make being around one any easier.

This book is going to give you all the information you need on narcissism, and it's also going to help you understand how to deal with one in your life. If you are in a relationship with a narcissist, it may be time to think of yourself and actually get out, if you find that you can't help them, or they don't want to accept help.

It's sad but true that many narcissists are actually very lonely individuals, lacking in self-confidence and not really understanding why people react to them the way they do.

So, whether you have a narcissist in your life, you think you yourself might have narcissistic tendencies, or you're simply interested in learning more, this book will give you all the information you need.

Chapter 1
Definition of Narcissist

In general, the simple definition of a narcissist is:

"Someone who has an excessive interest or admiration of themselves"

Of course, nothing in this world is ever that simple, because the world of narcissism is actually a deep and complicated well of personality traits and problems. The problem with that definition is that there are many people on the planet who are self-absorbed and a little 'too into themselves', but they're not necessarily narcissistic; they're just vain.

It is for this very reason that the term 'narcissist' is thrown around and attached to people who don't actually fall under the remit. In one way, this is a disservice to that person, because as you'll see as we go on to explore what narcissism really is, nobody wants to be labelled with this term if they truly aren't! On the other hand, it's a disservice to those who do suffer from Narcissistic Personality Disorder (NPD), because it's no joke, and it's not a choice either.

You see, as we go through this book, you're likely to start developing a deep-seated dislike for narcissistic people, but before you get to that point, I want you to think a little deeper. A person suffering from depression isn't blamed for their condition. A person with anxiety isn't laughed at for worrying too much. A person with an eating disorder isn't avoided and belittled. NPD is a real thing, a personality disorder, which therefore falls under the mental health umbrella. Any such condition doesn't deserve belittling, it doesn't deserve name calling or avoidance. If anything, we should be trying to help these people, but the problem? Most narcissists don't realize there is anything wrong with them, and they certainly won't accept your help willingly.

It's a doubled edged sword which has very few positive outcomes for most people.

This chapter is going to give you the basic points of what it means to be a narcissist. We're going to talk about the history of narcissism, the types of narcissists you'll encounter in your life, and the traits which embody a true narcissist. Remember, if you read one or two traits and recognize them in yourself or your partner, don't automatically jump to conclusions that you have NPD. Real narcissists embody several, if not all, of the common traits.

What is a Narcissist?

A true narcissist is someone who suffers from Narcissistic Personality Disorder (NPD) and is a person who has an extreme interest in themselves, an inflated sense of self-importance, and someone who struggles to maintain relationships and friendships with other people. It's likely that a narcissistic will not have long-lasting friendships in their life, e.g. they won't have someone in their life who they've been friends with since childhood, whereas many other people will have at least one.

The reason for this is that narcissists push people away with their behavior, although they don't actually mean to do it. You see, narcissists aren't trying to hurt people intentionally, they simply do it through their actions, and don't see anything wrong with what they are doing. A narcissist is never wrong in a narcissist's eyes. A narcissist's opinion is not an opinion, it is fact - that is how they see it.

We're going to talk about the traits of a narcissist shortly, which will bring more understanding in terms of what a narcissist actually is. We're also going to talk about NPD in far greater detail too.

For now, you need to understand that NPD is a very real condition and one which falls under the personality disorder umbrella. Just like someone with imposter syndrome, borderline personality disorder, or bipolar disorder, NPD isn't something you can snap your fingers and 'get out of', it is an ingrained part of who a person is. It can be mild, moderate, or it can be severe. It can be there all the time, or it can be flared up by experiences and situations.

The hope is that this book achieves the following two things, at the very least:

- Helping someone who is affected by a narcissistic relationship
- Helping to bring awareness to the fact that narcissism is a real thing

Narcissism in History

It might feel like narcissism has only become a 'thing' recently, but it's actually not the case. What is true is that narcissism seems to be a common buzz word at the moment, but the very idea of narcissism actually started way back in Greek mythology. In this form, Narcissus was a man who fell so deeply in love with the image of himself in the water that he simply couldn't stop admiring the reflection. He eventually died at the spot through lack of nutrition. From that point, narcissism has been considered negative.

Of course, in order for the idea of narcissism to have made it all the way to this day and age, there needs to have been studies and research continuing. The first such known study was in 1911, by Otto Rank. Freud also published a study on narcissism in 1914, before the groundwork for recognizing NPD began in 1967, through a study conducted by Otton Kernberg and Heinz Kohut. It wasn't until 1980 that NPD was officially recognized as a personality disorder, along with diagnosis criteria laid out.

Over the last decade or so, the word 'narcissist' has become common in society, but as we have already explored, it has been tagged to people who don't necessarily deserve it. True narcissism is very rare, and whilst people may occasionally exhibit narcissistic traits, perhaps even for prolonged periods of time, in order to be diagnosed with NPD itself, the story has to be a little deeper.

Types of Narcissist You Might Encounter

A narcissist is an individual kind of deal, just like every person is unique. There are several specific types of narcissist to know about. There are three main types to cover.

- **The Classic Narcissist** - You'll hear this type of narcissist also called the high functioning narcissist, the exhibitionist, or the grandiose narcissist. This is the classic category type that most fall into.

- **The Vulnerable Narcissist** - You will hear this type also referred to as compensatory narcissists, closest narcissists, or fragile narcissists. This type of narcissist will also feel that they are over and above everyone else, but they do not like being the center of attention, which pulls them apart from our first classic type. Instead of being in the spotlight, they attach themselves to other people who are of high importance, or who they perceive to be 'special'.

- **The Toxic Narcissist** - You will hear this type of narcissist called the malignant narcissist also, and this is the type that you need to be avoiding at all costs. This type of narcissist exploits other people for their own gains, and they are extremely manipulative. They seek out those who they assume to be vulnerable, e.g. empathic people, shy people, and they manipulate for what they can gain. This type of person craves control and in some extreme cases, may actually enjoy seeing someone else in distress or suffering.

Of course, every person you come across is unique and that means that a narcissist isn't likely to fall specifically under one type; they may exhibit traits of either type, but they will have one dominant category.

Traits of a Narcissist

Now we know what a narcissist is, and we know that there is a specific condition related to it, let's cover the main traits of a narcissist. Remember, there are three main types we have covered, and certain types will have specific traits, e.g. a toxic narcissist will be extremely manipulative emotionally, whereas a classic narcissist is more likely to be concerned with inflated ego, or thoughts of self-importance.

In general, however, the following traits are connected to those with NPD:

- An overwhelming need for attention
- Can often appear very charming at first
- Extreme jealousy
- Expecting special treatment and quickly becoming angry or aggrieved when it doesn't arrive
- An inflated sense of self-importance
- Often inflating the importance of talents or achievements
- Overinflating their abilities, often in romance and sex
- Very sensitive and easily hurt - doesn't handle rejection well and often responds with anger, shame, or extreme humiliation
- Has a hard time maintaining relationships which are healthy, either friendships or relationships

- Indulges in regular fantasies about their success, appearance, or power, etc.
- Has no problem taking advantage of another person in order to achieve something, and will not feel guilty about it
- Lacking in empathy, often disregarding the feelings of other people, even those close to them
- Considering that only 'special people' can understand them and how unique they are
- Often looking for positive reinforcement from other people or praise
- The idea that their opinion is right, and everyone else's is wrong
- The idea that everything they do is right, and they are never wrong about anything
- Assuming that everyone will agree with them or do what they want
- Only ever wanting the best of everything
- Selfish and arrogant

As you can see, there isn't a whole lot of positive there, and for someone who is in a relationship with a narcissist, they are likely to find the entire experience quite tough.

Is a Narcissist Actually a Bad Person?

When you read about narcissism and you read the list of traits, it's very easy to simply jump to the conclusion that a narcissist is actually a very bad person who should be avoided at all costs. The thing is, it's never that simple. Remember, NPD is a very real thing and is a personality disorder which falls under the mental health remit. You don't automatically judge someone who is suffering from depression for being detached, and you appreciate it to be part of their condition. The same kind of compassion should be placed towards NPD to some degree, however it is very difficult to do that when a person is treating you badly.

Some types of narcissists are easier to deal with than others, but if you are in the company of a toxic narcissist, you will find it extremely difficult to disagree with the idea that he or she is just a bad person.

Perhaps the best way to answer this question is to separate narcissists, or those who exhibit signs of

NPD into two camps - those who are trying to do good but end up being pulled back by their condition, and those who simply don't care about anyone else.

Every single person is unique and complex, and that means that you can't simply put an umbrella 'bad person' tag on everyone who has some degree of NPD; and remember, not every person with NPD has a full-blown version, some have a tinge of it, whilst others may experience it sometimes and not at others. Again, people are complex!

Chapter 2

Narcissist Personality Disorder and Treatment Options

We've talked about NPD a lot in passing, but we've not really delved into what it is and what causes it. This chapter is going to do exactly that.

We know that NPD is a personality disorder, and these types of conditions fall under the very large mental health umbrella. Most people consider depression, anxiety, stress, and schizophrenia as the only types of mental health condition, but the list is far longer than that. For instance, bipolar disorder, borderline personality disorder, eating disorders, etc.; these are all mental health conditions in their own right.

Personality disorders are a sub-category of mental health issues, and people with these types of disorders have unhealthy thoughts and thinking patterns, and they also have behavioral issues too. These types of thinking patterns are often very rigid, and it can take a large amount of therapy to challenge and change these patterns over time. Most people with personality disorders also have problems relating to and perceiving people and situations.

What Causes NPD?

Nobody really knows. It's not an easy question to ask what causes any type of mental health issue, even depression. Some people are more prone than others, and in the case of NPD, some people have it and others don't; some people have just a little and other peoplc have a full-blown case. It's a mystery in some ways, but many studies suggest that the following issues may be risk factors for developing NPD in later life:

- Hereditary issues, e.g. genes, particularly those which have an impact on the connection between behavior and the brain, e.g. oversensitivity
- Negative experiences in early childhood, e.g. abuse or poor parenting techniques
- Psychological issues

- A large amount of criticism experienced
- Previous trauma
- Having unrealistic expectations

Narcissists are not born, they are made. Whilst genes play a part, it is thought that experiences have a greater influence on the development of NPD at any age. Of course, it doesn't happen over-night, but NPD can occur at any age. For the most part, however, it begins in childhood, due to nega-tive experiences and as a result of poor parenting practices, such as being insensitive as a parent, or from over-pampering and over-praising.

The Diagnostic Criteria for NPD

Diagnosis of NPD can be difficult, and because most people with this condition don't really seek out help for it (most don't think there is anything wrong with them), then many practitioners don't really have a huge amount of experience in offering a diagnosis. What is more likely to happen is that a general practitioner (regular doctor) will refer someone with this type of problem to a mental health practitioner. From there, in order to be diagnosed with NPD, a person will need to **meet five (or more) of the following criteria**:

- An exaggerated sense of self-self-importance
- A believe that they are special and should only be associated with high-status individuals
- A need for excessive compliments and admiration
- An exaggerated sense of entitlement
- Takes advantage of, or exploits, other people
- A lack of empathy
- A believe that others are jealous of them, and also struggles with jealousy themselves
- Arrogance on a regular basis

The Actions and Thoughts of a Narcissist

Getting into the mind of a narcissist can be a difficult thing. Every person thinks and acts differently, and every person is unique in how they approach situations and react to them. A narcissist, on the other hand, has some specific behavioral patterns, which makes them stand out. Whilst there will be anomalies here and there because everyone is different, there are two main examples to look at.

Using Either Overt or Covert Methods

In order for a narcissist to manipulate a person or situation, so that their needs are met above everyone else's, they will use methods which are described either covert or overt. Overt methods are quite obvious, whereas covert methods are quite secret and go under the radar. The covert methods are often the most destructive to other people, and this is why many people who are in relationships with narcissists often struggle to leave; they start to question 'is it me or them'. A classic method here is called gaslighting, and we'll cover that in far more detail a little later on.

Generally speaking, a classic narcissist is always going to use overt methods, and a vulnerable type of narcissist will use covert methods. The problem is that toxic or malignant narcissists will probably use a clever mixture of both.

A Somatic or Cerebral Approach

This is about how a narcissist appreciates things, and themselves. A narcissist using somatic methods will be completely taken by the way they look, their body, and their general appearance. They will be extremely vain. A cerebral method, however, is using the brain, and appearing to be overly intelligent; this type of narcissist will go to great lengths to convince you that their opinion is indeed the only one we'll be taking any notice of.

It's important to try and identify the type of narcissist you're dealing with, and whilst that can sometimes be difficult to pinpoint exactly, you will certainly be able to identify the most dangerous type. A toxic or malignant narcissist will have no issue in hurting others and will show no remorse. This type of narcissist is damaging to everyone around them, and it's likely that a person who escapes a relationship with this type of narcissist will need emotional support, and possibly therapy, afterwards.

Of course, you might read this and wonder how a person can't see that there is something wrong with the way they are acting and thinking, but that is exactly what NPD does. Remember, NPD is a personality disorder, which creates a disordered way of thinking. A narcissist will 100% genuinely think that you are in the wrong, and that you should be seeing their uniqueness, that you shouldn't be arguing with them because they're right. They won't look at themselves and consider that maybe they're wrong, or maybe they could have dealt with the situation better; a true narcissist doesn't see an issue in the way they think or the way they act. In the case of a toxic or malignant narcissist, this type of person certainly sees no problem in hurting another person for their own gains either.

Why Most Narcissist Never Receive Treatment

The last paragraph should answer the question of why most narcissists don't seek out treatment. Most narcissists don't realize there is a problem, and if someone tells them they need help because they're showing narcissistic tendencies, they're likely to laugh and turn it around on the other person.

Of course, this isn't the case for everyone, and for a person who may have a mild case of narcissism, there might be a light bulb moment when they think 'hey, I wonder if that applies to me', when reading an article or after someone has pointed out that they're acting in a narcissistic way. This is a rarity, however, and it's extremely unlikely that a classic or vulnerable narcissist of the truest type will seek out help.

Will a toxic or malignant narcissist ever get help? In some cases, this does happen, but usually only after a rather self-destructive moment, or when they have hurt someone else extremely badly. If an extreme moment pushes them to a certain point, it may be that medical help is recommended, and possibly accepted. Despite that, it's still unlikely, and that in itself is a very sad fact.

Can Treatment be Successful?

There are many different types of treatment for NPD, but most of it centers around behavioral changes and challenging thought patterns. In some cases, extreme cases, hospitalization may be recommended, especially for extremely toxic narcissists who have driven themselves to a very self-destructive moment.

The problem is that most treatment tends to center around solving the incident, rather than solving the actual condition.

So, can treatment be successful? It can, when help is sought, but it takes a huge effort and commitment on the part of the narcissistic party. Treatment also isn't easy, and the same goes for any type of condition which requires cognitive behavioral therapy and challenging mindsets and thoughts. This isn't a treatment method which will be successful overnight and will require a long-term approach, with probably maintenance treatment beyond that.

Other Personality Disorders Related to Narcissism

Most personality disorders and some mental health issues are linked together in certain ways. For instance, a person who suffers from depression may also suffer from anxiety, because there is a close link. A person with stress may suffer from anxiety, for the same reason. A person with bipolar disorder may also have links with narcissism, and a person with a borderline personality disorder may also have NPD too.

Despite that, there are three main types of personality disorder which also link closely with NPD in particular:

- Antisocial personality disorder

- Borderline personality disorder
- Histrionic personality disorder

An experienced healthcare professional will be able to assess whether the specific type of personality disorder at large, however again, convincing someone to seek out help can be difficult, especially someone with NPD.

Chapter 3
Common Narcissistic Situations You May Encounter

Up to this point, we've talked about what narcissism is and we've described it, but in order to really show you how it affects people in real terms, we need to give a few examples and scenarios.

This chapter is going to talk about possible situations in friendship, family life, relationships, and working environments, where narcissism may play a part. Remember, these are only examples, but they highlight how narcissism is usually played exhibited in real life. We'll highlight the narcissist's point of view, and how it makes the other person/people feel too, to give a complete picture of the problem.

In these scenarios, you might feel that we're focusing on men, but it doesn't actually matter which gender the narcissist or other party is, it's more about the actual scenario and actions/thought processes. Despite that, there are a higher percentage of male narcissists on the planet than female.

Friendship Situations

<u>Scenario 1</u>

Two men are friends, one of which is a narcissist (undiagnosed). They haven't known each other for too long and simply met through acquaintances at work. They are sat talking over a drink one evening, discussing politics. The narcissist gives his view of the situation, speaking over everything which the other person says, and laughing whenever the other friend tries to argue a point. In the end, the narcissist simply labels his friend stupid for not understanding his view, and 'how it really is'.

- **The narcissist's view** - The narcissist cannot understand why his friend wouldn't see his point of view as valid and starts to wonder why he is even friends with this man if he can't grasp basic intelligence.

- **The friend's view** - The friend feels hurt and annoyed that his so-called friend called him stupid and wouldn't even listen to his view. He now considers his friend extremely arrogant and starts to wonder whether he should continue spending time with him.

Scenario 2

Two women are friends, however, one friend (non-narcissist) always feels belittled by the other one. This particular day they decide to go shopping together because there is a big party coming up and they both need new outfits. The narcissistic friend chooses an outfit and walks around the dressing room in a sense of self-importance, lapping up compliments from everyone. The other friend tries a dress on, but the narcissistic friend belittles her with a comment about how it doesn't suit her and turns the conversation around to how great her dress looks.

- **The narcissist's view** - The narcissist thinks she looks fantastic in her dress and wants everyone to tell her so. She also needs everyone to tell her so, to give her the confidence to buy it.

- **The friend's view** - The friend is upset that she didn't pay any attention to what she was wearing and threw an offhand comment about it not suiting her. She felt disappointed and hurt, but then, it's always that way.

Family Situations

Scenario 1

A brother and sister are visiting their parents for Sunday lunch. The brother is narcissistic. Instead of allowing his sister to tell their parents what she has been doing that week, the brother talks endlessly about his week and how he impressed his manager. Every time his sister tries to interject, he simply dismisses her talk and continues his own tale.

- **The narcissist's view** - His sister's week was average and not worth talking about, he was full of success and he wants to share it with his family.

- **The sister's view** - Yet again her brother isn't letting her talk about her achievements, even though she was really proud of the presentation she gave at work that Wednesday. She simply keeps quiet and lets him talk, as always.

Scenario 2

Two brothers are helping their parents move to a new house and they come across several boxes of old things from their childhood. One brother's box is in the way of the other brother's box (the narcissistic brother's box is at the back). Rather than simply moving it out of the way, the narcissistic brother kicks it to one side, thus landing in a large puddle of garage oil. He pushes it with such force that it falls over and everything lands in the oil. The other brother's things are therefore almost ruined, but the narcissistic brother doesn't even bat an eyelid - he was head boy at school, so his childhood photos are more important.

- **The narcissist's view** - He wanted to get to his box of things to relieve his wonderful childhood achievements. He knows that his other brother didn't come anywhere near to his achievements, so what's the point in looking in his box?

- **The brother's view** - He is angry that his things are now ruined, and that his brother considers his childhood memories and belongings to be more important than anyone else's. This then results in a fight which he will never win, because his brother isn't even listening.

Relationship Situations

Scenario 1

A man and a woman are in a relationship which is almost reaching the year-long mark. The woman is going out for the evening with her friends, to celebrate a birthday. She comes downstairs wearing a dress, feeling really happy with the way she looks. Her boyfriend (narcissist) laughs at her and tells her the dress makes her look 'dumpy' because she's so short. Her good mood disappears, and she decides not to go out as a result. The boyfriend then suggests they spend the night in together because he wants her 'all to himself'.

- **The narcissist's view** - He didn't want her to go out because there were going to be too many men in the room and people would look at her in a short dress. He's instead happy that they're going to watch a film together and order a takeaway.

- **The girlfriend's view** - She thought she looked great and expected her boyfriend to compliment her but as soon as he told her she didn't look good, she lost all interest and confidence. She stayed in because if she had gone out anyway, she knew he would have been in a bad mood when she returned home. What's the point anyway?

Scenario 2

A woman is on her phone in the living room, idly scrolling through Facebook and checking her messages. She is smiling at something she has just seen on her Timeline. She puts down her phone and goes to the toilet. Her boyfriend (narcissist) wants to know why she was smiling, assuming that she was messaging another man. He takes her phone and because he knows the passcode, he looks at her messages. He sees a message from someone called 'David'. He immediately flies into a jealous rage, demanding to know who David is. David turns out to be her cousin, asking how her mum is.

- **The narcissist's view** - She has been smiling at her phone and engrossed in it for the last half an hour, she must be doing something. Who is David? How could she cheat on me? He basically flies into a jealous rage, not taking the time to actually read the message.

- **The girlfriend's view** - Completely offended that he thinks she would cheat in him, especially as she was doing nothing wrong. He's always like this, always jealous over petty things. He won't say he's sorry and she knows it.

At Work Situations

<u>Scenario 1</u>

A narcissistic woman works in an office and is always trying to make friends with management. She doesn't bother to speak to her colleagues or spend time with them, she would much rather try and become closer to those who she seems to be 'worth her time'.

- **The narcissist's view** - Management understand her and how special she is, they understand her potential and she is going to achieve. Why should she bother spending time with those below her?

- **Her colleagues' view** - She's always trying to get on side with management, it makes us all feel sick. Why does she think she is so special?

Scenario 2

In a brainstorming session, one employee (male narcissist) suggests something which he believes to be the answer to the entire problem at hand. His colleagues simply note it down but don't give it much praise. The narcissist cannot believe that his colleagues can't see how fantastic his suggestion is. Instead of wasting time, he goes to his manager and explains his idea instead, not bothering to wait for the final outcome.

- **The narcissist's view** - The idea he just came up with is perfect, why can't these people be able to see that? He believes that his manager understands him better anyway, so he goes to talk to him and puts his idea forward.

- **The manager's view** - Although the manager appreciates employees' ideas, and he has an open-door policy for suggestions, the employee displayed a certain air of forced authority which didn't come over as very welcome to the manager. The manager can't understand why the employee didn't simply allow the idea to be noted down with everyone else's and discussed as one.

As you can see, these scenarios point out some of the common narcissistic traits that you'll see in everyday life. Whilst you'll see these types of examples from general people who might be acting in a slightly narcissistic way, it doesn't mean that they are a narcissist! As we've mentioned several times, someone who wants praise doesn't necessarily fit the bill for narcissist diagnosis; they might simply be lacking in confidence at that time and want a little extra support. A person who acts in a jealous way over his girlfriend one or two times isn't necessarily a narcissist, they might be feeling insecure in the relationship due to a problem.

It's important to see the bigger picture, rather than simply jumping to conclusions and assuming that you are dealing with a narcissist. What these examples do however is show you just how annoying and upsetting a narcissist can be when they do things which belittle or upset someone close to them.

Working with a narcissist isn't easy, that's for sure. You'll find that narcissists try and enamor themselves with managers and those in authority because their inflated sense of importance leads them to believe that they are simply paying their dues in the office/another workspace, and that they are soon going to be promoted to a higher level anyway. In addition, a narcissist will push their ideas over everyone else's, and probably stamp over anyone who gets in their way.

What we haven't mentioned is the possible scenarios of a very damaging type of narcissist - the toxic or malignant narcissist. These types of scenarios can be very damaging and very dark indeed. For instance, emotional abuse at the hands of a narcissist of this type can be extremely mentally damaging to a person. This can be a family member, friend, relationship partner, or manager. Being constantly belittled, beaten down emotionally, and made to feel like everything is your fault can push someone towards a mental breakdown.

As we've mentioned before, and we'll certainly mention again in our next chapter, being in a relationship with a toxic or malignant narcissist is a form of abuse. The person won't notice it at the time, they'll be convinced it's them doing something wrong, purely because the narcissist is telling them that (gaslighting).

It doesn't have to be a relationship, it can be a parent who is narcissistic to this degree towards their child. In this case, the child is very likely to grow up with severe trauma and have issues of their own throughout their adult life. This in itself is likely to cause the toxic narcissism trait to continue onwards and taint that child's life in the years to come.

Whilst narcissism can simply be annoying, it can also be extremely dark and damaging too.

Chapter 4
How to Survive a Narcissistic Relationship

Most people are open to the idea of meeting a partner and having a healthy, loving relationship. This is what most people aim towards, and even if it isn't your final aim in life, most of us enjoy the process. What we don't enjoy is meeting someone who is unable to have that kind of healthy relationship.

A narcissist finds it extremely difficult to maintain healthy, loving relationships. The reason isn't clear, and it can vary from person to person; it could be because they experienced a lack of affection when they were a child, it could be because they've been hurt before and as a result they are using defense tactics, or it could be because they exhibit very jealous traits which make it borderline impossible for another person to live with. Of course, there is also the rest of the narcissistic spectrum of traits to take into account, which makes it very difficult for someone to maintain a relationship in a healthy way, with someone who has NPD.

When we meet someone we like, we know that there is a chance we are going to get our heart broken, and whilst we hope that it won't happen, we know that it is a possibility. We try not to let this bother us and simply move on with the fun side of a relationship. The problem is, a narcissist doesn't have the right amount of empathy or trust for a relationship to be anything but chaotic and emotionally damaging for the other person. As a result, many narcissists end up alone in the long-run. Most partners eventually leave, because they simply can't take it anymore; it can be a mild reason, or it can be something more severe, such as emotional abuse and gaslighting techniques.

We've mentioned gaslighting a few times already, but if you're not sure what it is, we're going to cover that in more detail in this very chapter. Whilst gaslighting isn't only found in narcissist relationships, it is quite common in this type of union.

We also know that there are more male narcissists on the planet than women. In that case, it's more likely that the male partner will be narcissistic towards the female, but that shouldn't lead you to believe that it is never the other way around. Just as there are many relationships which involve emotional abuse from the female partner to the male, there are also female narcissistic relationships too, either same-sex or female to male. People are people at the end of the day, and a narcissist is a narcissist whether male or female.

What most people don't understand about relationships with narcissists is how it actually got to the point of being a relationship in the first place. Surely if someone is being treated badly from the start they would leave before emotions got involved? Let's explore that in more detail.

A Wolf in Sheep's Clothing

One way to describe a narcissist in a relationship is like a wolf in Little Red Riding Hood. The wolf was clever and dressed up as someone Red could trust, i.e. her grandmother. By doing that, he appeared to be something he wasn't. Many narcissists do this without even realizing it.

When you first meet a narcissistic in a potentially date-like or attraction situation, they will be on their best behavior. He or she will be as charming as can be. Nobody really knows why this is the case, but it is thought to be down to their deep-seated desire to be liked and approved of. When they see someone they like, their desire is to potentially 'own' that person. Not in the actual ownership sense, but in a 'look what I managed to attract' kind of way. It sounds terrible, but that is how the mind of a narcissist operates at the first signs of attraction.

When a man or woman meets someone, who is on their best behavior, charming the socks off them and complimenting them on everything they say and do, it's hard not to become enamored. It's also worth pointing out that certain types of narcissists, especially the toxic ones, tend to focus on those who are a little emotionally weak or vulnerable.

This makes the first stages of attraction far easier to navigate; someone who is quite vulnerable is probably going to overlook a few red flags, compared to someone who is strong and has a high level of self-worth. In that case, a person is far more likely to walk away at the first sign of an issue.

Once that first flush of attraction begins, the narcissist will keep up the wolf in sheep's clothing act until their partner is totally hooked. By that point, all bets are off. By that point, the true colors start to show.

This is why so many men and women end up in relationships with narcissistic partners. They have been tricked by an illusion.

Of course, not every narcissist is like this; we are painting a picture of the very worst type of narcissist here. Having said that, it is a common way for people to become close to those who do have narcissistic traits. In addition, it could be that an empathic person, or someone who has a natural tendency to want to help others, see the damaged side of a narcissistic and wants to make them 'better'.

You cannot make a narcissistic better. You cannot change them and heal them, but it doesn't stop some people from trying. One of the most toxic combinations in romance is a narcissist and an empath, and it is for this very reason. We're going to cover that particular subject in a little more detail shortly.

Signs You Are in a Relationship with a Narcissist

If you're in a relationship currently and you're looking at your partner and thinking 'you might be a narcissist', or you simply want to know what to look out for in the future, let's check out some of the most common signs that you are indeed in a relationship with a narcissist.

- **He or She Hijacks Every Conversation** - If you're out on a date, or you're simply chilling at home, and he or she always turn every conversation around to themselves, you're looking at narcissism territory. Narcissists love to hear their own voice and they love to talk about themselves and what they've done. If you manage to get a word into the conversation, then it's likely that whatever you say will be ignored or thrown to one side. When you start talking, they will probably interrupt you and turn everything back to themselves.

- **Showing Off on Dates** - Whilst it's nice to be wined and dined if you notice that your partner goes out of their way to basically show off when they take you out, it could be a narcissistic nod. Do be careful with this one, because it could equally be your partner trying to woo you! A few signs to look out for include tipping far too much, not tipping at all, treating the waiter with disrespect, or ignoring advice on wine/food from the waiter and telling them that he/she knows better.

- **Always Breaks Promises and Oversteps Boundaries** - If he or she is always borrowing things and not bringing them back, maybe borrowing money, or simply avoiding the need to recognize your personal boundaries, then that is a narcissist sign to look for. A narcissist doesn't have respect for anyone else's thoughts or feelings, because they have very little empathic ability. They also don't know much about personal space, so if you find that they're always 'in your space', that's something to look out for too. If they make you a promise and barely keep it, again, red flag.

- **Everything is Your Fault** - They make you a promise or say they'll do something and when they don't do it, they turn the blame onto you. For example, perhaps you were supposed to meet for coffee after work but he or she didn't turn up. A response could be 'what do you expect, you didn't remind me!'. They might be cooking dinner and burn it, and it will be your fault because you distracted them with something you said.

- **They're Always Looking in The Mirror** - Whilst many men and women have slight vanity issues, narcissists are literally in love with their own appearance. If you notice that your partner is always looking in the mirror, always changing their hair or dress sense to look good and gain approval from others, then narcissism could be on the cards. A narcissist has to be the best, look the best, and be admired, and they place a huge amount of importance on appearance over everything else.

- **Your Opinion Isn't Worth Anything** - If you're having a conversation about something and you voice your opinion, a true narcissist will belittle that view and tell you that you're stupid/your opinion is stupid/tell you that theirs is better. Trying to get a narcissist to agree with you is a blatant waste of time and oxygen.

- **They Have to Have the Best** - Possessions and the way others see them is vital to a narcissist. For example, if you're trying to buy a car together but you're on a budget, a narcissistic would rather go down the finance route and land themselves in debt to drive the latest Mercedes, than go for something lower in status quality, but within budget.

- **They Matter, You Don't** - A narcissistic partner will expect you to forget your wants and needs and focus entirely on theirs. If anything, your wants and needs never registered on the scale! You will, therefore, need to drop every-thing for what they need, and they will not show any thanks in return.

- **Arguments Often End in Them Sulking or Running Away** - Narcissists do not handle re-jection or criticism well, in fact, it will end in them either sulking and starting another argu-ment or running away/becoming emotionally detached. This can extend to a certain type of emotional abuse also because by belittling you in the middle of an argument, they make them-selves feel better about the criticism you've given them (probably rightly).

- **They Often Act Out of Jealousy** - Narcissists are often quite jealous and this is even more so in a relationship. If you notice regular bouts of jeal-ousy, then that is a narcissistic red flag to be aware of.

How many of those signs you see in your relation-ship depends on whether or not you can truly class your partner as narcissistic. Don't go throwing the label around just because you can tick off one or two! Remember, in order for a narcissist to be diagnosed with NPD, they need to tick five or more of the traits from a rather short list, as outlined in the diagnostic criteria. We can't give you a definite number of these signs to tick off, but you would be looking at half or more, over a constant period of time, before you could categorically decide either way.

Is There a Future for a Relationship Touched by Narcissism?

Ah, the million-dollar question. We cannot say yes, and we cannot say no, it really depends on the couple and the amount of narcissistic involved.

What one person is happy to put up with, another person would run away from. What you need to do, however, is ask yourself whether you're truly happy and whether you see a future for the two of you. Never stick with a narcissistic person if they are making you feel unhappy, belittled, or questioning your own self-esteem or sanity. The problem is, that questioning your own sanity is part of the whole gaslighting issue we've mentioned so many times already.

Many men and women stay in narcissistic relationships because they aren't sure whether or not they're imagining it, or whether it's really happening. Deep down, they know something isn't right and they know that they shouldn't be dealing with the way things are, but they love that person, and they don't want to give up on them. Whenever their partner shows their bad side, they quickly show their good side not long afterwards; by doing that, they're keeping the person right where they want them - not leaving.

In terms of whether there is a future or not, perhaps we should instead be questioning whether there is a *healthy* future or not. There is a difference between a general future and a healthy one. A relationship where one partner is constantly belittling and dragging down another isn't healthy, whether they're doing it because of a personality disorder or not.

There aren't that many narcissists who remain in relationships for that long. The reason is that in the end, the other partner really sees the light and finds the strength to leave. This doesn't always happen, and there are instances where a future could be on the cards, provided the narcissistic partner is able to realize that they are doing and get help. It does happen, but it doesn't happen often.

Whilst we might be painting a bleak picture, it really is a case of looking at your individual circumstances and deciding what is right for you. There is no right or wrong answer here.

The Narcissist and The Empath

There is one particular toxic mixture that we need to talk about in more detail. This combination of people is a highly damaging and extremely incompatible one, but it is also a very common union you will find. We are talking about a person classed as an empath and a narcissist of any type.

For this to be a damaging combination, the narcissist doesn't have to be a toxic or malignant type, they can be classic, vulnerable, or a combination of types. The problem here is that an empath is an extremely sensitive person, someone who is hurt easily and who wants to help. A narcissistic possesses very little, probably zero, empathy and as a result, the two cannot understand each other. You might wonder in that case how they come together in the first place, but it is a union which is surprisingly common.

The bottom line is that an empath wants to help, and they are attracted by the charming nature of a narcissist when they first meet. Whilst empaths usually have extremely good instincts and can normally spot someone acting out of character from a long distance, a narcissist is extremely good at getting past that defense mechanism. As a result, the empath finds themselves totally enamored with this new person in their lives. They then start to see chinks in their armor, e.g. the vulnerable side, the side which needs constant reassurance. The empathic side of their nature then wants to help, and almost wants to 'fix' the narcissist.

As we've explored already and will certainly delve into in more detail later in the book, a narcissist cannot be fixed, as this is an ingrained part of their personality which requires professional assistance in order to change the disordered pattern of thinking. What eventually happens is that the empath is belittled and emotionally damaged by the narcissist's lack of empathy and general behavior. It's also likely to be the case that an empath will struggle to leave the narcissist because they will keep turning on the charm just at the moment, they think the empath is finally going to summon up the courage move on.

Empaths are extremely sensitive, as we have already said. They do not understand how someone can use emotions for manipulation and they are extremely easy to hurt. Therefore, the thoughtless actions of a narcissist can cause extreme upset and hurt to an empath.

Of course, the same could be said for any type of emotionally sensitive person. In many cases, narcissists actually seek out vulnerable and sensitive people, because they are far easier to manipulate. This is particularly the case with toxic and malignant narcissists, who almost seem to get a kick or some kind of enjoyment out of causing distress and upset to another person.

Unfortunately, the only way to get around this particular problem is for an empath to see the light and leave. For many people, however, that is extremely difficult and pulls on every heart string possible. Even when someone does bad to an empath, they still try and see the good in them.

When it's Time to Leave

Whilst it's not impossible for a relationship touched by narcissism to succeed over time, there are far more instances when the union will ultimately fail. It is likely to be a long and protracted process, because of something which we're going to finally get around to discussing next - gas lighting.

The person in the relationship with the narcissist will question themselves endlessly and wonder whether they really are being treated badly, or whether they are imagining it. The narcissist will turn everything around on them and make them feel like it's them that is to blame. For a person who is quite sensitive or emotionally vulnerable, this type of treatment can cause them to stay in a relationship which is damaging and unhealthy for far too long.

A person leaving a narcissistic relationship will probably go back a few times before finally breaking contact. A narcissist is unlikely to just 'let it go'. As we've mentioned previously in this book, many narcissists want to have the best of the best, and they collect things as possessions. In some ways, their partner is an extension of that. When their partner chooses to leave them, they see this as a failure and a huge rejection. They will react either with anger, or they will attempt to charm them back, reverting to the 'old' version which initially attracted the person to them in the first place. In many cases, this can be enough to get their partner to return to them because they still have deep feelings underneath it all.

Many partners who leave this type of relationship require a large amount of support afterwards, and some even require emotional counseling. Depending upon the type of treatment they have been subjected to (far worst in the event of being close to a toxic or malignant narcissist), the empath may find it extremely difficult to have trusting and healthy relationships in the future, without some kind of therapy or support into the future.

As you can see, narcissistic relationships aren't just damaging for the narcissist (because many ends up missing out on genuine loving unions as a result of their inability to have healthy relationships), but also for the partner too. Leaving it difficult, and in some cases, it can be a process which takes months, if not years.

It's often the case that they know their partner is narcissistic towards the end. This is usually the catalyst for making them think they should leave.

However, when gas lighting begins, the difficulty really turns itself up a notch or two.

So, let's finally get around to it - what is gaslighting?

Understanding Gas Lighting

First, let's define the term.

To gaslight or gas lighting, is to psychologically manipulate someone into doubting their own sanity.

This is a classic narcissistic move, and it is something which all types of narcissists use from time to time. It can be mild, moderate, or it can be extremely severe. In the case of being emotionally abused by a toxic or malignant narcissist, gas lighting can cause the partner to feel like they are actually going insane.

To really highlight what gaslighting is in practice, let's look at some of the classic techniques used by narcissists, which all add up to the same thing - gas lighting.

- **Withholding** - The narcissist will refuse to listen to their partner or pretend that they simply don't understand what they're saying. They will do this by twisting things, e.g. 'here we go again, you just keep saying the same things', or 'I have no idea what you're talking about'.

- **Diverting or blocking** - This can include telling their partner that they're simply imagining it, that it's not happening and they're creating it in their head. It can also include changing the subject so that their partner doesn't get a chance to air their problem or views. For instance, 'you're imagining it'.

- **Countering** - In this case, the narcissist will make the partner question their memory of something that happened, even though they have it perfectly clear in their own mind. For instance, 'you never remember things properly, that didn't happen'. The partner then starts to question whether it really did happen or not.

- **Denial** - This is when the narcissist will make their partner question whether something really did happen. This is likely to be the case when the narcissist promised to do something and didn't. Rather than admitting that they forgot, they will say 'I don't know what you're talking about', and pretend it never happened.

- **Trivializing** - This is a common form of emotional belittling, whereby the narcissist places no importance on the way their partner feels, or their needs. For instance, 'you're far too sensitive'. 'I can't believe you're upset about something that small'.

These five techniques are classic gaslighting methods, and they can be used all at once, in separate sequences, etc. How a narcissist uses gas lighting entirely depends on the situation, but they all add up a form of emotional manipulation which can, in the end, cause the partner to stay with them when they deep down know they should leave; this happens because the partner starts to wonder whether it really is them making things up and seeing things that aren't there, or whether their instinct is right.

The doubt is often enough to make them stay but remain unhappy.

It's important that your understanding of gas lighting is really clear because this type of emotional manipulation really adds up to abuse. It's so subtle that a person often doesn't realize they're being subjected to it. If you're not sure if this is happening to you, ask yourself the following questions:

- Do you constantly doubt yourself, always second-guessing?
- Do you ask yourself if you're too sensitive on a regular basis?
- You feel confused on a regular basis, and sometimes wonder if you're going crazy
- You're always the one saying sorry, even though you sometimes think you shouldn't apologize
- You know that you're unhappy and you can't really understand why
- You're always trying to make excuses for the behavior of your partner to those close to you, e.g. friends or family

- You often don't tell your friends and family about things that have happened
- You have a gut feeling something isn't right, but you have far too many doubts to act upon it
- You start to pull yourself back and act in a different way, even lying, to avoid situations which you know are going to be twisted
- You look back on the past fondly, remembering when you were far more fun-loving and relaxed
- You often feel that you can't do anything right
- You start to question your ability to be a good partner

If you're thinking these things on a regular basis, there is a very good chance that you are a victim of gaslighting by a narcissistic partner. The importance of recognizing this is so great that we can't emphasize it enough. People who are being emotionally manipulated in this way cannot see it because gas lighting is very successful. It is subtle enough to go undetected but strong enough to work.

Let's further reinforce this subject with a few signs that you are in a relationship with a narcissistic partner, who is using gas lighting as a manipulation technique.

- **They lie a lot, to your face** - You know they're lying, but the lies are so blatant that you can't help but wonder whether it's a truth. This is about keeping you off-balance, so you are never really sure what the truth is.

- **They always deny that they said something, even though you know they did** - Even if you have a text message from them saying a specific something, they will deny it and even deny the proof exists. It starts to make you question reality too. The more they do it, the more you start to believe that their side of the story is right.

- **They use those close to you** - A narcissist might use your family and friends, those they know are important to you, and say nasty things to damage your self-esteem. For instance, if you have children, they might turn around and say: "you shouldn't have had your children you're not a fit mother". This means their emotional attack hits deep.

- **You can see the pattern over a long period of time** - Gas lighting never happens quickly, and it is always a long, drawn-out process which digs deep over time. It will start slowly, e.g. the odd lie or remark, and then it will gain momentum. The fact it starts in this way means that a partner will rarely notice it until they are in the grips.

- **They don't do as they say** - The whole 'actions speak louder than words' analogy is clear here. If you can look at what your partner is saying and see that it doesn't match what they are doing, this is a subtle gaslighting technique. Remember that words mean nothing if they're not backed up by reinforced actions.

- **They use positive words and actions too** - If someone was gaslighting you on a negative level all the time, you would see it; in this case, a narcissist will revert back to their old charming self, and compliment you, to confuse you into thinking that you're imagining all the bad things. For instance, they will belittle you and make you feel worthless about an opinion or something you did, and then they will praise you for something else. This means that the power balance is always in their favor, and they know that confusion is always going to be an element in you staying and not leaving them.

- **They tell other people you're crazy, or you** - If your partner is always telling you that you're crazy, or they tell other people that you are, that is gas lightning because it's surely going to make you question your own sanity.

- **They make you believe that everyone else is lying, or to blame** - This is another method to make you question your own sanity and wonder who is actually telling you the truth. The end result is probably that you alienate yourself from those around you, and the only person you have is the narcissist themselves.

The main point of highlighting these common examples is to help you quickly become aware of whether or not a narcissist is actually gaslighting you. See how many of these you can nod your head to. Remember, it's not a definite sign of gas lighting if you can only tick one off, and it only happened once. Everyone is a little manipulative from time to time, it's part of human nature; however, if it happens on a regular basis and you can agree to several techniques, that could be a very real sign that this form of emotional manipulation is actually happening to you.

We've mentioned that the term 'narcissist' is far too often thrown around these days and that real narcissism is actually rarer than most people think, on the other hand, is extremely common, but we should point out that it's not only used by narcissists. This is a form of emotional abuse which can be used by anyone who wants to manipulate another person. It has roots in narcissism, and most narcissists (all types) use it. Be on the lookout for these types of techniques coming your way and be sure to spot the red flags before they become too ingrained. Remember, it's not your fault, and you're not going crazy.

Dealing with Emotional Abuse

The problem with emotional abuse is that the person who is being abused is often clueless that it is happening. That all comes down to gas lighting, and the fact that the narcissist has used is to so slowly and subtly, that it has crept up on them without them even noticing it. By the time they start to question what is really happening, and perhaps someone else makes them aware of it, getting out of the situation has become very difficult indeed.

Emotional abuse is never okay, and it is not something you should stick around and cope with. The title we have used, i.e. 'dealing with emotional abuse', isn't about coping with it and staying in the same situation, it is about to understand it and getting out of it in a healthy way, to minimize future effects on your emotional and mental health.

Emotional abuse often flies under the radar and isn't given the same amount of shock factor as those who are victims of physical abuse. This is probably because there are no physical scars to see; you can't see the scars that someone inflicts emotionally, they can only be felt. The thing is, physical abuse heals, and whilst it certainly leaves mental scars, finding support is usually an easier process. Society has made it far more difficult to seek help for emotional issues; we tend to recognize what we can see. Hopefully, in the future, that will change, but the tides are turning and there is a lot more recognition of emotional abuse as a damaging factor than ever before.

Over time, emotional abuse can cause a person to question their entire sanity, making them live with cripplingly low self-worth and self-confidence. They will become house-bound, alienating themselves from those close to them and avoiding anything socially minded. This is not a happy or healthy life.

The following steps will help you deal with the emotional abuse that a narcissistic relationship may be throwing your way.

- **Identify What is Really Happening** - First things first, you need to be honest with yourself and see things for what they truly are; you are being emotionally abused by a narcissist. Yes, you may love this person, but this relationship is not healthy for you, and you are the main concern here, right now.

- **Make Your Own Health a Priority** - Your mental and physical health should be the most important thing on your mind right now. Stop trying to please your partner, and instead turn your attention inwards. Make steps towards increasing your confidence, perhaps by finding a new hobby or starting the gym and boosting your health and confidence. Practice self-care and allow yourself to heal, before making positive, affirmative steps.

- **Set Yourself Boundaries** - It's vital that you set boundaries with your partner. Tell them that they cannot shout at you like that, they can't insult you, they can't call you names. You should also tell them that if they continue to do this, you will leave. If they do it again, simply walk out of the room. It's vital that you follow through on these boundaries.

- **Stop the Blame Game** - Anyone who has been subject to emotional abuse at the hands of a narcissist will probably send a large proportion of their day blaming themselves for everything that goes wrong in the relationship. This needs to stop. Ask yourself this very painful, but very real question - why would someone who claims to love you act this way? Yes, they have a condition, but does this mean you have to suffer? No. You cannot control the situation, so avoid blaming yourself for it.

- **Be Very Clear in Your Own Mind That You Cannot Fix Them** - Do your research into NPD and be very clear that you cannot fix them, so don't even try. You can attempt to have a conversation with them and perhaps highlight the fact that you suspect they may have NPD, but a true narcissist is probably going to throw that idea right out of the window and blame you for suggesting it. You're going around in circles and it's time to break the chain.

- **Build up a Network of Support** - Confide in someone you trust about the reality of your situation and do not feel ashamed or guilty about it. The more support you can muster, and it is out there, the easier it will be for you to gain perspective and become strong enough to make your final step.

- **Walk Away** - Sounds easy, but it's not in practice. Put together a plan which allows you to walk away from this abusive relationship with your head held high. Know in your heart that your partner will try to pull you back, but that is the whole point of putting together the support network we mentioned in our last step. Be strong and know that you do not deserve to be abused, by someone who has a condition or otherwise.

- **Seek Help if You Need it** - It's not a weakness to ask for help, and if after you've finally broken the relationship you need to speak to a professional in order to work through the issues you've faced, then do it. Most people who have been in these types of relationships do need some kind of therapy or counseling afterwards, in order to build their self-confidence and sense of self-worth once more. By doing this, you're investing in your future, when you meet someone who truly does deserve your kind heart.

The hardest thing about NPD is that it is a personality disorder and therefore a mental health condition. We know that a person doesn't do this by choice, but they also don't choose to seek help and fix it either. Know 100% that there is nothing you can do, know that you deserve better and that although you love this person, they are never going to be what you really need and deserve.

Why Narcissists Are Often Lonely People (Although Won't Admit it)

The fact that we've spoken in detail about the fact that a person in a narcissistic relationship will probably need to leave, tells you a lot about why narcissists are often lonely people. The problem is, they won't admit this. They will tell you that the people who have walked out of their lives weren't worthy of their time or attention anyway. Their sense of grandeur stops them from seeing that they treated someone special very badly, or that they perhaps were at fault for them leaving in the first place.

It's a sad fact, but most narcissists end up alone, and those who do go on to have relationships are often poor relationships which aren't at all healthy. Of course, it's not a 100% certainty that a narcissist will be lonely, because some do go on to have brighter futures, but in order to do that they need to seek help and counseling to overcome their personality disorder and be able to, therefore, have healthy and meaningful relationships in their lives, to the benefit of both sides.

Chapter 5
Helping Someone with Narcissism

You might wonder why we are going to talk about how you can help someone with narcissism when we have spent so long telling you that you can't fix them. That isn't the point. We're not suggesting that you can wave a magic wand and fix this person, allowing them to have meaningful and lasting relationships and friendships, we're suggesting that there are ways you can at least help someone, and maybe encourage them seek help.

Know right now that it might not work - narcissists are by their very nature very stubborn and are not going to accept help if they don't deem it to be strictly necessary. By suggesting that they may have a problem and need help, you are (in their eyes) attacking their very personality and self, and that will not be taken lightly.

Narcissists aren't always 100% narcissistic; you might have someone who only has narcissism when certain events trigger it, e.g. when they're rejected or go through a hard time, and as a result, their personality disorder comes to the fore. On the other hand, you might deal with someone who is narcissistic all of the time, but not to a huge degree. These are the types of people you may be able to help, but anyone who is 100% severe and toxic in terms of narcissism, don't even bother trying to help. These people will not take your suggestion well, and the only way that these types of narcissistic will ever receive help is when they take everything a step too far.

How Can You Help a Narcissistic Person?

So, in what ways can you actually attempt to help a narcissistic person?

There are very few ways you can change anything, but you can try and encourage them to seek help by subtle moves. Again, this depends on the type of narcissism they are experiencing. You should also be very prepared for rejection of your point but know that at least you tried. From there, you can figure out your own options and decide what your own plan of action is going to be. Remember, you can't change someone else without their will to want to change, you can only control yourself.

There are three main ways you can attempt to help someone close to you who is clearly in the grips of NPD.

Do Not Allow Them to Manipulate You

This particular step is for you mainly, but it does help them indirectly. By refusing to let them manipulate you, by allowing their gaslighting attempts to backfire, you're actually making them sit up and take notice. They will see that you are stronger, and they will wonder why. They will not want you to leave, they need you around, even though their behavior probably shows otherwise.

Of course, in order to not let them manipulate you, you need to be aware that emotional manipulation is going on in the first place. The steps we talked about in our last chapter, in terms of how to deal with emotional abuse, will help you in this regard. Set boundaries and tell them that the way they are speaking to you isn't acceptable and that you will simply walk away when they do it. In addition, make sure if you say you're going to do something, you actually do it.

In some ways, dealing with a narcissist is like dealing with a child. If you tell them they can't have something, but then give in, they'll simply continue that level of behavior because they know you'll give in at some point. Narcissists will do the same thing, which is why it is so important that if you say you're going to walk out of the room when they belittle you, you actually do it. Do not apologize for something that isn't your fault and do not bow down to their demands.

This will take practice and it will be hard, but by looking after yourself and your own needs first, you will find the strength to be able to do it.

By ensuring that their tactics backfire, you're taking away a huge amount of their power. This could go one of two ways - they could turn angry and simply lash out at your attempts, or they could possibly start to soften. It depends on the level of narcissism they are affected by. Of course, if they lash out, cut your losses and walk away. You've tried, and there's nothing more you can do.

Wait Until They Are Calm, And Have a Discussion

If you've tried step one and it didn't go too badly, e.g. they soften a little, then perhaps this second step may help. Remember, in order for someone to seek help, it has to be their decision. It's no good forcing someone to see a doctor for anything they don't believe is wrong with them. Think about an alcoholic, for instance, you can't force them to see a doctor and admit that they need help - the first step towards recovery is knowing that there is a problem in the first place.

The types of treatment for NPD all hinge on total commitment to the treatment at hand. If someone doesn't really believe they need this help, the treatment isn't going to work at all. So, the point of this step is to simply sew a seed in their mind and help them explore the possibilities.

Wait until they are calm and sit down and have a conversation. Be soft and don't be forceful. Talk to them, not at them, and make sure that you keep your emotions level. Tell them that you feel like they're treating you in an unfair way and give examples to back up your words. Tell them that you know they don't mean to treat you this way and that they are a good person. If they remain calm, you may be able to make progress. If they simply throw a narcissistic tantrum and turn it around, again, you can't do anymore.

Find some literature on NPD and leave them on the table. Tell them that you've found this information and perhaps they might like to read it. Suggest you can read it together, or they can read it on their own, and that you'll be by their side whatever they decide.

Remember, it's not 100% guaranteed that this step will work, but it's worth a try if you want to know you did all you could before you decide whether or not to walk away. It's also important that if by some stroke of luck, they do agree to perhaps talk about things with a health professional, and that they recognize there might be something not quite right, then you remain supportive and on their side at all times. Remember that deep down a narcissistic is lacking on confidence and needs constant reassurance. The fact that you've suggested there might be something wrong with them could go either way, but by being soft and supportive, being on their side at all times, you may be able to guide them through it and towards professional help.

Issue an Ultimatum

This is the final method to try, and it's not one you should attempt as a first port of call. This is not likely to go well, but there is a chance. By issuing an ultimatum you're basically saying 'look, I do not want to be treated in this way, but I know it's now what you really mean to do deep down. I'm giving you one chance to sort this out, and I will be by your side all the way. If you refuse, and if you continue to act in this way, I will leave for good'. You have to go through with your ultimatum and do not attempt to go back on it. Be strong and see it through, whichever way it goes.

The point of this, however, is not to shout and lecture, it's a firm statement of intent. If you add emotions and hysterics, they are not going to take you seriously.

These are the only ways you can attempt to help someone with NPD, without actually being a health professional. Even if you were a health professional, the person would need to be willing to seek help and make a commitment towards really putting in the effort to change. Treatment for NPD is quite intensive and requires a lot of deep thinking and behavior change. This requires a strong will to make it work, so you can see why someone who is being forced to seek help is not going to have a good outcome.

The Importance of Knowing You Cannot "Save" Anyone

We've said this once, and we need to say it again. You cannot 'save' a person with NPD, and you cannot fix them. This intention can only come from themselves. It's sad to walk away from someone who has a condition and doesn't actually 'mean' to act in a certain way, but at the same time, you can't wave a magic wand and make it all go away again either.

The only thing you can do is focus on yourself and go with what you feel is right. You know in your gut that you deserve happiness and if your partner/friend or whoever this person is to you is not going to give you that, the only thing you can do for yourself is walk away. If you are in a relationship with this person, what would happen if children came into the equation? Would you want them to be born into a relationship that had a large narcissistic element? That is certainly something to think about too.

Make sure that you have this fact in your mind before you attempt to help someone with NPD, and before you make a decision to walk away. By knowing that in a solid and firm manner, you won't have regrets about your final actions.

Are Narcissists Dangerous?

The final thing to address in this chapter is to talk about whether narcissists are actually dangerous people.

The answer to this is wide-ranging and it really depends on the person. Is a toxic or malignant narcissist dangerous? Yes. Perhaps not physically so, but certainly emotionally dangerous and mentally abusive. This type of narcissistic has no problems with manipulating another person; to give you an idea of how bad this can get, a toxic narcissist will stand there and laugh when their partner is having an emotional breakdown and crying because of something they've said or done. These types of narcissists are cruel, so in that way, yes, they are dangerous; dangerous to someone's mental and emotional wellbeing.

Dangerous physically? We can't generalize but on the whole, no. Having said that, toxic narcissists are sometimes linked with psychopaths and sociopaths, and there are many triggers which can send that type of person over the edge and towards extremely dangerous behavior.

If we're talking about a classic or vulnerable type of narcissist, the danger is more likely to be subtle and emotional, rather than physical. Remember, emotional abuse is just as bad (if not worse) than physical abuse, and just because you can't see the scars, it doesn't mean they're not there.

Dangerous for your future happiness? Definitely.

Chapter 6
After You Walk Away

If you do have to walk away from a narcissistic partner, friend, family member, etc., then there are a few things you need to know about 'after the event'.

It's this simple - a narcissist is not likely to shrug his or her shoulders and say, 'okay then, see you', and then let you walk away with nothing else occurring. It's far more likely that they will revert to their best behavior and try and lure you back.

There is one very good reason for this - because they hate rejection and take it very badly indeed. When you walk away from a narcissist you are rejecting them as a person, no matter how badly they treated you. They will not see all the emotional abuse and manipulation that came your way, in their eyes, they treated you like a king or queen. Instead, they will see you walking away, and it will rile them, or cut deep into their self-conscious depths. The next step could be one of two things:

- They will either become angry and resentful and probably bombard you with messages and social media posts about how they're better off without you and you're this, that, and the other (more abuse)
- Or they all become the epitome of charm once more and try and remind you of all the good times

If you find scenario one coming your way, ignore and block. This is simple pride getting in the way. In this case, they see you as rejecting them, they see you as making a mistake, and they're turning the whole thing on you. Of course, you know better. Block their number, block them on social media, do not go anywhere you know they will be, and go and stay with a friend for a while if you're worried, they're going to turn up at your door. Eventually, they will become bored and grow tired with no response. Sad, but true.

Scenario two is also common, and this is how many people in narcissistic relationships end up going back time and time again. The only answer here is to stand firm and remember why you left. If you can stick with your tried and tested support group, then even better. These people will remind you when your resolve might be wobbling, and it will at some point. You did have good times, and you were with them for a reason. Remember, if you've been a victim of gaslighting then it might also be that you're unsure of your next step because you're still suffering from the after-effects of this type of emotional abuse. Your friends and family will need to hold you firm in this case, but again, block numbers and social media access. The less they can contact you, the easier it will be for you to make large strides into your future.

What to Expect:
- Begging
- Pleading
- Bargaining
- Blame games
- Insults

- Eventual silence

If you think you're out of the woods then the silence comes, don't be so hasty. If they see you in the street quickly afterwards, bargaining and pleading is likely to start again. Breaking away from a narcissist takes time but know that it will be a process you'll be pleased you embarked on.

Dating After Leaving a Narcissist

Once you are over the 'getting away from a narcissist' process, the future will seem brighter and far clearer. It's important to give yourself the time to grieve the relationship properly, and not to jump straight into another union in order to try and block out the upset that occurred previously. This is a common scenario, but more common is trying to avoid another relationship altogether.

Remember that you cannot judge a future partner based on what you went through before, but it's entirely normal if you do. For this reason, seeking out counseling or therapy after leaving a narcissistic partner is a good idea. By not dealing with everything that happened, you are actually putting your future at risk. Many people who have emerged from narcissistic relationships are so scarred by what they went through emotionally, they don't want to ever get close to another person again. As soon as a new partner starts to show even the tiniest hint of something which could be akin to narcissism, they run.

The fact is that we all show slight signs of narcissism from time to time, but that doesn't make us narcissists. We can all lack empathy sometimes, we can all belittle someone without meaning to once or twice, and we can all act in ways we wish we hadn't. The difference is that we will apologize and see the error of our ways, whilst a narcissist won't. Do not make the error of labelling everyone with the same tag or tarring everyone with the same brush.

The best way to dip your toe back into the dating world after emerging from a narcissistic relationship is to do so slowly. Try this:

- Give yourself time to simply be. Don't attempt to do anything, don't try and feel anything and don't push yourself to move on; simply spend time on yourself and try and unpick the events in your mind and deal with them. If you need to gain someone else's perspective, or you need to seek out professional help, now is the time to do so.

- Focus on yourself. Next, it's time to seek out things you enjoy and be kind to yourself. You spent so long with someone being unkind to you, it's likely that you've forgotten how to do things for yourself and to enjoy them. Find a hobby you've always wanted to try, go to a night class, go out with friends, spend Sunday mornings being lazy, read your favorite books, eat your favorite foods, and get out into nature.

- Focus on your health. Next up, after your self-focusing time, turn your attention to your health. A healthy body and mind are the best types of revenge! Whilst revenge shouldn't be on your mind, being a better version of yourself after a bad experience certainly feels great. Eat healthy foods, make sure you get plenty of exercise, get plenty of sleep, avoid stress, and make sure that you challenge your mind on a regular basis. You will notice how much stronger you feel.

- Enjoy your life. Once you start to feel better, and it may take considerable time in some cases, simply start to enjoy your life. Don't make it your sole aim to meet someone, and don't even think about dating; if it happens, it happens. There is plenty of time for all of that.

- When you're ready, simply be open to the possibility. The point is to try and meet someone who is worthy of your time and attention and who can give you what you didn't have before. The point isn't for someone to complete you or heal you. When you think you might be ready, simply be open to meeting people, but don't place huge importance on it. People who have come out of narcissistic relationships can sometimes be needy because they're so desperate for it not to happen again. By following these steps and placing importance on building yourself up once more, this is far less likely to happen to you.

- Do not tar them with the same brush. Again, if you do meet someone and you start to date, don't tar them with the same narcissistic brush as your ex. This is a vitally important step. True narcissists are very, very rare, and that is something to remember. It's highly unlikely you're going to meet someone with NPD twice in your lifetime, and whilst it's possible that you might meet someone who acts a little narcissistic on occasion, this isn't at rue narcissist and therefore won't bring the same types of problems.

- Know the signs. Do not run at the first sign of a problem but always hold your requirement for respect and understanding high up on your list. If someone starts to treat you badly, address the issue and stand firm before walking away. If being in a relationship with a narcissist will teach you anything, it's not to allow the same thing to happen again.

If you're reading this and thinking 'there's no way on Earth I'm even attempting to date again, I'm good by myself', it's time to question why you feel that way. Are you saying that because you truly don't want a relationship and you would rather be alone and spend your time traveling, making meaningful connections with friends, etc? Or, are you saying it because you're scared of going through the same thing twice?

Some people don't want to be in a relationship and that's fine, provided it's for the right reasons. If you're avoiding romantic connections simply because you're scared, that's something to address early on. You will probably find that your feelings change over time, but avoid being closed off to possible connections, simply because your past experiences are clouding your judgement.

Remember, you deserve to be loved, no matter what you might have been forced to believe in the past.

The Future for a Narcissist Who Refuses Help

We've talked a lot about the future for a person who was in a narcissistic relationship, but what about the future for the narcissist themselves?

It doesn't paint a great picture if the person isn't willing to seek help. In that case, it's far more likely that a narcissist will end up jumping from destructive relationship to destructive relationship, and if they do end up in a long-term union, it's unlikely that their partner will be truly happy and fulfilled. That person is far more likely to be simply 'putting up' with the narcissism.

If a narcissist ends up in a relationship which yields children, the sad truth is that their children are quite likely to develop narcissistic tendencies as a result of being open to them during their early years. Whilst there isn't a certain answer in terms of what causes NPD, there a definite suggestion that childhood experiences have a very firm link towards someone developing the personality development in their adolescent and then adult years.

Narcissists also have a habit of becoming quite bitter over time. This is partly because people have come into their lives and then left them, and they can't see why; of course, they will project the blame onto the other person and won't see their role in them leaving. Many narcissistic traits, therefore, worsen with age, as more experiences are racked up throughout life.

As you can see, it's quite a bleak picture we're painting and that is the sad truth about life as a narcissist. People will only stand being treated a certain way for so long before they eventually pluck up the courage to leave. Whilst some may never get to that point, these relationships are likely to be empty and lacking in true love and respect.

For these reasons, the biggest price a narcissist pays for their actions over time is loneliness and a lack of truly meaningful relationships in the end.

For a narcissistic, however, the most loving and deep relationship they have is with themselves.

Are Modern Social Elements to Blame?

You're almost at the point where you know everything there is to know about Narcissistic Personality Disorder and the traits and issues which go alongside it, but we also need to explore one possible area before we sign off. Are modern social elements to blame for the rising number of narcissists in the world?

Remember, true narcissists are quite rare, yet it's a term that we hear on such a common basis. For that reason, perhaps narcissistic tendencies are becoming more common, and we have to question why that is. Is it down to the social pressures we are forced to deal with? Is it down to social media? Is it because of pressures to be the best, look the best, and own the best?

It's probably unfair to lay the blame of narcissism at the feet of modern society, but you have to wonder whether it has played a hand. For instance, social media has made us all so much more aware of other peoples' lives, and our appearances. Social media influences are always telling us that if we want to be the best, we need to look the best, and that means using this product. We're bombarded with people taking selfies and full body photos, without realizing that they've been photoshopped and filtered to within an inch of their lives. Most of what we see these days simply isn't real. Is it any wonder that we have such high and unrealistic expectations of what we're supposed to be, what we're supposed to look like, and what we're supposed to aim for?

We aren't entirely sure what causes NPD, so could it be the things we're exposed to in modern life? Of course, much of NPD is thought to be down childhood experiences, but what influences those experiences? What causes a person to act a certain way, causing trauma to another, which could then lead them to develop a specific type of personality disorder? It's hard to pinpoint, but you have to consider the possibility if nothing else.

Whilst we may never entirely understand what causes NPD, and there will always be a certain amount of stigma attached to it, trying to be the best is always a fruitless task. Perhaps instead we should simply be aiming to be ourselves.

In terms of future generations, perhaps it is our responsibility to ensure that children are raised to be happy with who they are, without the need to continually compete and reach certain unrealistic goals. By doing that, we will raise a generation of youngsters who are well-mannered, respectful of others and fulfilled. Surely those are major boosts towards avoiding personality disorders and the types of trauma which may contribute towards development.

Conclusion

And there we have it! We've reached the end of our book about narcissism, and by now you should be far clearer about what it is and what it really means.

After reading this book you should bandy around the idea of narcissism far less and appreciate that it is actually a truly rare personality disorder which shouldn't be misinterpreted. A person who is a little jealous or unkind once or twice in their life isn't a narcissist, they're simply having a bad day; provided they realize this and apologize to those they offended or hurt, there is no harm done. If however, that person doesn't see a problem with their actions, you could be dealing with someone who has an NPD touch.

Whilst a narcissistic cannot actually 'help' what they do, that doesn't mean that you should stick around and put up with it if they're not willing to seek out help to change. Leaving a narcissist behind isn't easy, but it is entirely necessary in order to live a happier life in the future.

The sad thing about narcissism is that whilst we're always talking about it in a negative way, the person who is truly affected is the narcissist themselves. This person is going to end up lonely unless they seek out steps towards a brighter future. This doesn't happen often however, because most narcissists don't realize there is anything wrong with them, and they assume that everyone else has the problem, not them.

Points to Take Away from This Book

Now you've read everything we've had to say about this rather confusing, yet fascinating subject, what are the main points to take away from the book?

- Narcissism is far rarer than most people think, with just 1% of the population affected on the whole

- True narcissism means being diagnosed with Narcissistic Personality Disorder (NPD)
- Men are far more likely to be narcissistic than women, however, that doesn't mean that female narcissist don't exist!
- A narcissistic is defined by a sense of the grandeur of one's self, inflated ego and self-importance, and a need to be the center of attention, but the traits are quite far-reaching beyond that
- Narcissistic behavior can be mild, moderate, or extremely severe
- Many narcissists use emotional abuse without even realize it, e.g. gas lighting
- There are several types of narcissists, including classic, vulnerable, and toxic
- Toxic or malignant narcissists are extremely damaging and are closely linked to psychopaths and sociopaths
- Many narcissists end up alone in the end, because they refuse to see a problem with their actions, and blame everything on those around them

- A person in a relationship with a narcissist is likely to be subjected to various levels of emotional abuse and manipulation, and will probably find it very hard to leave
- Empaths and narcissists are the worst combinations on the planet
- Treatment for Narcissistic Personality Disorder (NPD) involves therapy, counseling, behavioral therapy and challenging mindsets, and can take a considerable amount of time
- There is no known cause for NPD, however, it is thought to stem from childhood, and could be genetic

- Underneath it all, narcissists are fragile and lacking in self-confidence, with a need for constant validation
- Narcissists take rejection extremely badly
- In order for a person to receive treatment for NPD, they need to realize the problem for themselves, and this cannot be done for them. For this reason, most narcissists are never diagnosed and never treated

- It is impossible to fix or change a narcissist without them seeing the error of their ways and understanding that they have a personality disorder which requires treatment
- Finding the strength to leave a narcissistic relationship can be extremely difficult, and many people need to seek professional help afterwards, e.g. therapy and counseling
- Gaslighting is a very common tool employed by narcissists, which involves manipulating the thoughts and emotions of another person, causing them to question their own sanity
- You should never feel guilty or bad about needing to leave a narcissistic relationship - it's important to focus on yourself

There is a huge amount to talk about on this subject, and we've covered the main areas in detail, whilst reiterating the key points several times. Because narcissism and emotional abuse are so closely linked, this is a subject which requires a lot of press space. There is no fun in being in a relationship with a narcissist, just like there is no fun in a friendship with a narcissist or being closely linked in a working situation. All you will deal with is constantly belittling and their inflated sense of grandeur. Despite that, it's also important to realize that this person isn't a 'bad person', they're someone who is suffering from a personality disorder, which actually links very closely to other mental health problems.

By knowing all you can possibly know about narcissism, you can take the right steps towards managing a situation which is touched by narcissism in your own life.

The takeaway point from this whole book? If a narcissist tells you it's your fault, it's really not. Never feel guilty for putting yourself first.

Extra

If you enjoyed reading this book, please, check the other manuscripts of the author:

Emotional Intelligence

A Complete Guide to Mastering Social Skills, Improving Your Relationships, Controlling your Emotions and Raising Your EQ

Would you like to master social skills and build better relationships? Would you like to improve your communication skills? Would you like to better understand your emotions?

If your answer is yes, this book is what you need!

In today's life, social skills have become more and more important. We often see people with excellent work skills being obscured by others who are less gifted, but who have a better ability to relate to others.

In this complete guide, you will learn all the knowledge necessary to improve your social skills, obtain the desired results in your life and increase the EQ.

You will discover:

- An analysis of emotional intelligence and its aspects
- How to build your emotional intelligence to improve all aspects of everyday life
- How to **improve your motivation** and have a positive attitude
- Practical and feasible **exercises to increase your EQ**
- How to understand your emotions
- Advices on **how to manage stress and anger**
- Causes of everyday problems and how to best deal with them
- How to deal with manipulative people
- **...and much more!**

Every step we take in life, every move that we make is influenced at some point by our emotions. When you find it difficult to manage your feelings, that's when situations start to become a real challenge.

All charismatic and successful people have a great ability to recognize and control their emotions, and therefore maintain the composure needed to make appropriate decisions.

Emotional Intelligence has come to be known as the most important ability for all humans. It can help you in most areas of life. With it, you will be able to build stronger relationships and achieve personal and career goals without getting bogged down by social mistakes and obstacles. Instead, you will be able to avoid such obstacles and learn from your mistakes in social situations. This is all thanks to being aware of yours and others' emotions and the outcomes of certain behaviors.

Victor Murphy

Cognitive Behavioural Therapy

An Effective Guide for Rewiring your Brain and Regaining Control Over Anxiety, Phobias, and Depression

Suffering from a mental disorder you have probably already heard about CBT – Cognitive Behavioral Therapy. Even if you haven't you will learn now how this type of therapy can change your life. You will finally be able to say goodbye to all those days when you felt anxious and depressed. Your life will again work in harmony.

CBT is one of the best tools used by therapies and it is based on a very simple idea. Because of its simplicity, you can practice CBT yourself in the comfort of your home. However, in order to do this, you will need this book to guide you through the process.

First of all, you need to get educated about your mental disorder. This will help you to determine how to approach it with more precision. Well, think about it, how can you work on something without first learning about it?

In this book, you will get a simple guide that will help you to use CBT to fight depression, anxiety, and phobias. With patient and everyday work, you will finally win the fight.

Now it is time to stop your negative thoughts, start practice mindfulness so that you can be aware of the sensations happening inside you and in the environment around you. Learn how to form goals and how to organize so that you can achieve them. Goals forming are also the base of good structure CBT session.

So, in this book:

- Introduction to CBT
- How to stop the Negative Thoughts
- Becoming more self-confident
- Forming Goals and achieving them
- Mindfulness as a powerful tool against depression, anxiety, and phobias
- Applying CBT and simple exercises

Victor Murphy

Empath

An Effective Guide to Understanding and Developing Your Gift. Overcome Fears & Use Your Potential

Do you experience countless emotions within the space of one day? Are people always telling you that you're 'too sensitive?' Do you often feel overwhelmed and experience the need to run away from social situations?

If you're nodding your head, there is a very good chance you are an empath.

This is good news! You're one of life's good guys, you're a true Earth Angel, and someone who has massive potential to help others and create a lasting legacy in the world. What you need to do however is learn how to harness that potential and develop your gift.

Empath: An Effective Guide to Finding Yourself and Developing Your Gift is the ideal book for anyone who has empathic tendencies. Not only will you find all the information you need on what an empath actually is, but no stone is left unturned in terms of how to overcome potential challenges and develop your gift to its full potential.

You will discover:

- How to Develop Your Gift
- 7 Reasons Why Being an Empath is a Gift
- Characteristic of Empathic Peoples
- Why Empaths have a Better Ability to Help Others
- How to Use Your Potential
- Quick Quiz to Determine Your Empathic Status
- Spiritual Healing Tools to Help You as an Empath
- **...and much more!**

From learning how to ground yourself to visualization techniques, meditation to self-help, Empath teaches you how to handle the negative energies that come your way, giving you the space to focus on the positives instead.

There is no doubt that being an empath is a challenge, but all it takes is the right information and know how to turn it form a challenging situation, to a hugely positive and special situation instead.

There is no need to be overwhelmed or confused for a second longer, download this book today, and look forward to a brighter future, free of empathic burnout and over-sensitivity.

Victor Murphy

36555638R00073

Made in the USA
San Bernardino, CA
22 May 2019